ANTI-STRESS COLORING BOOK

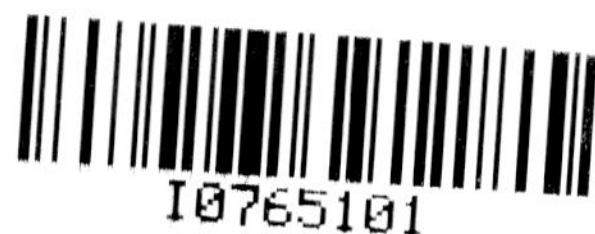

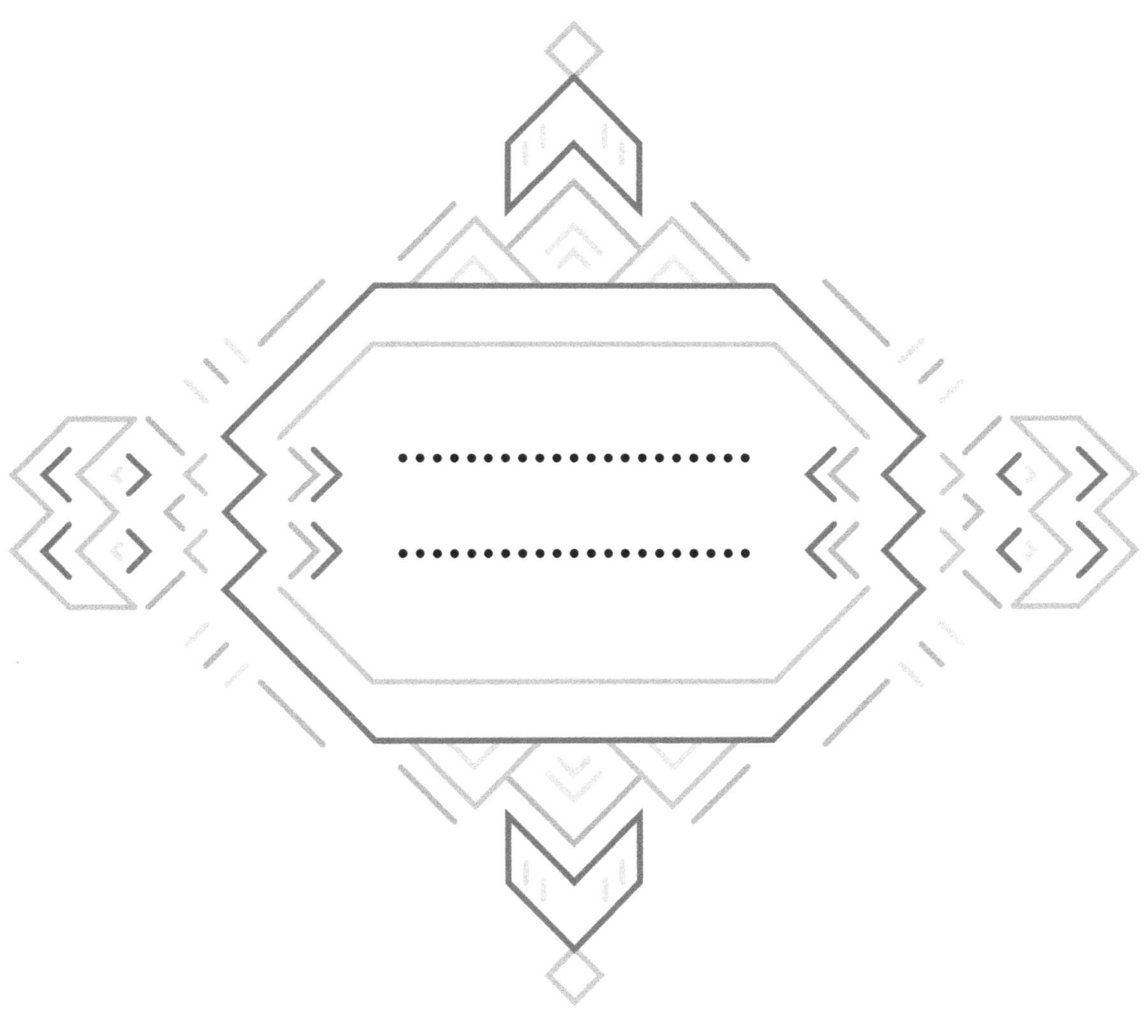

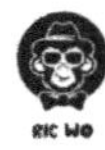

VOL 7

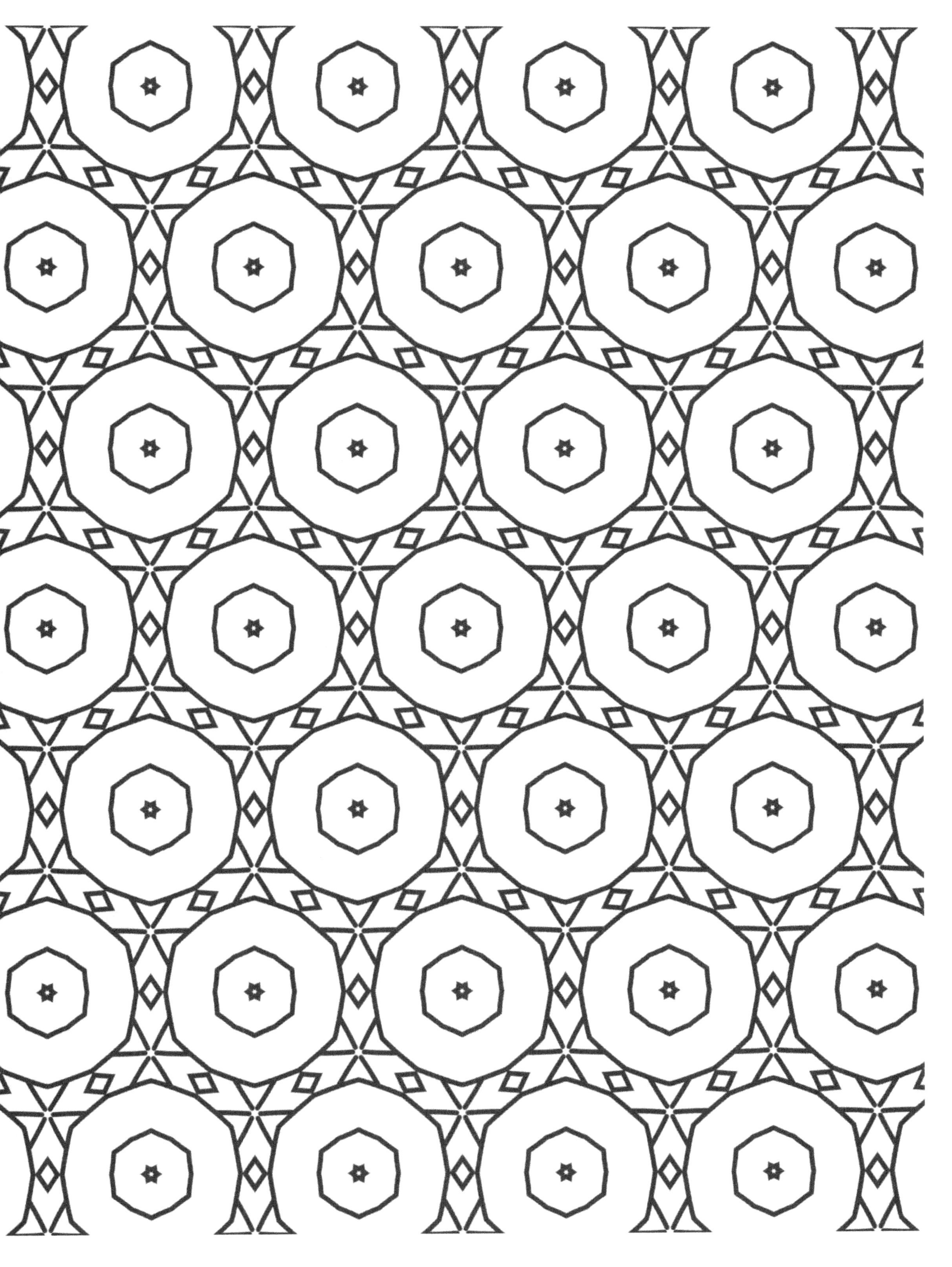

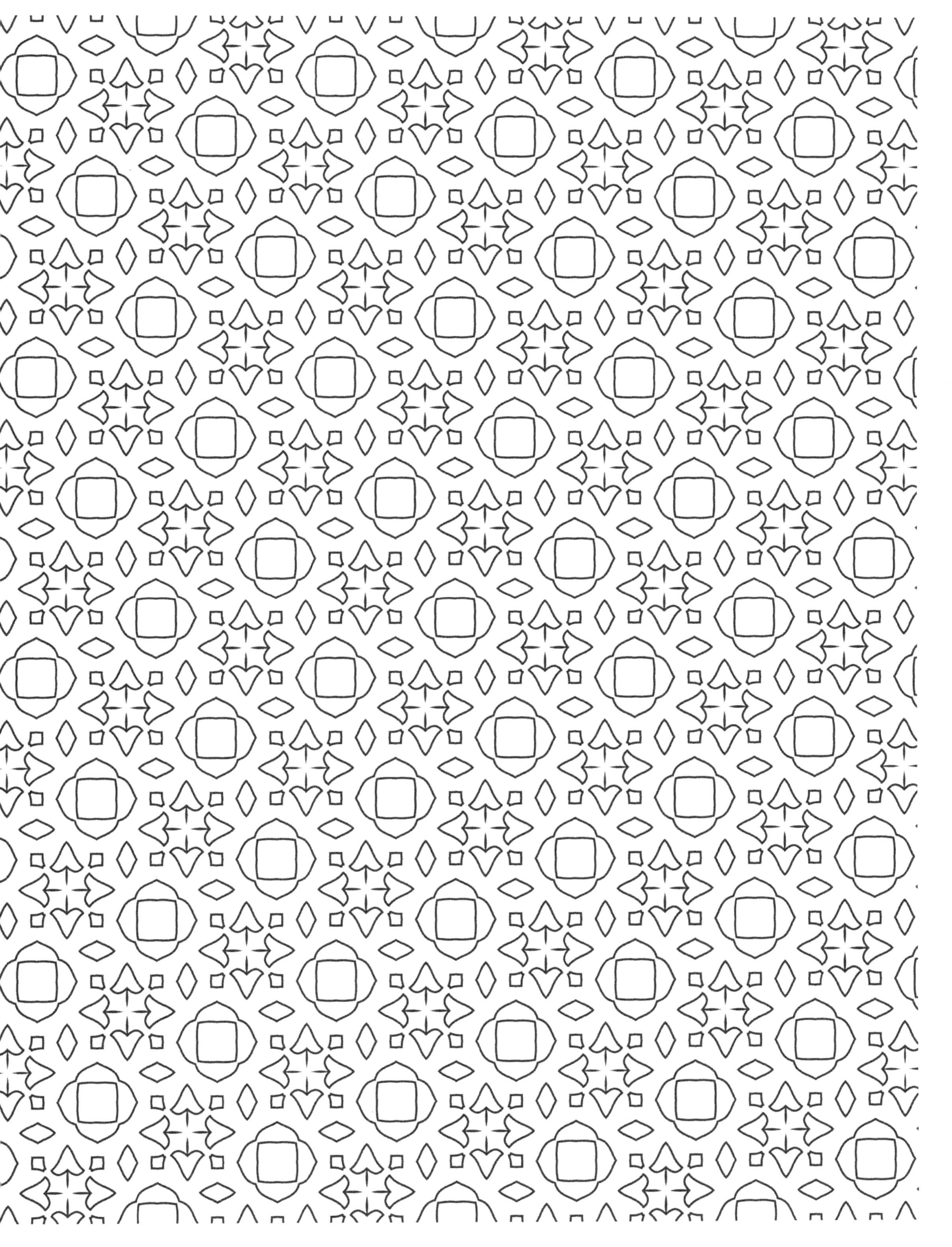

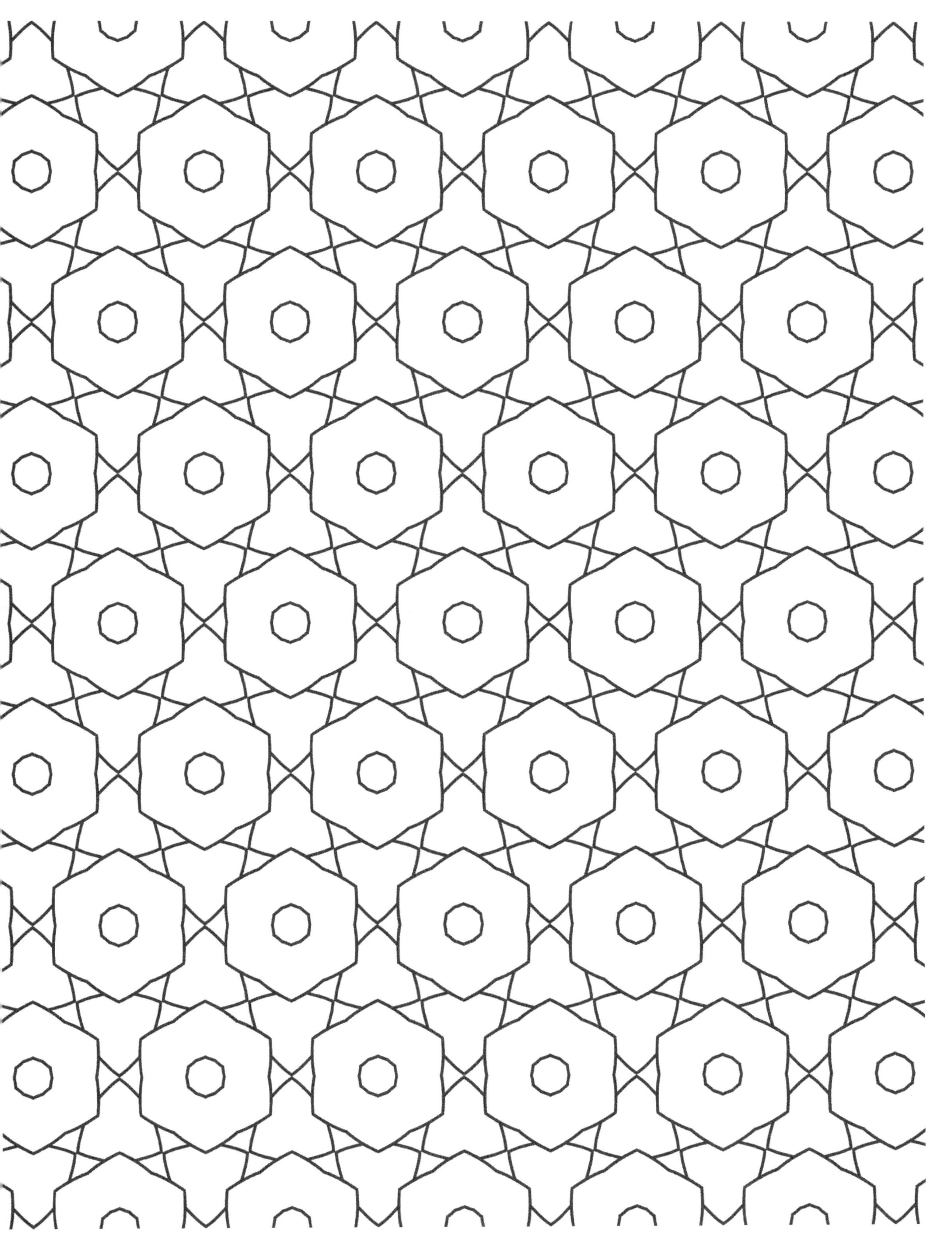

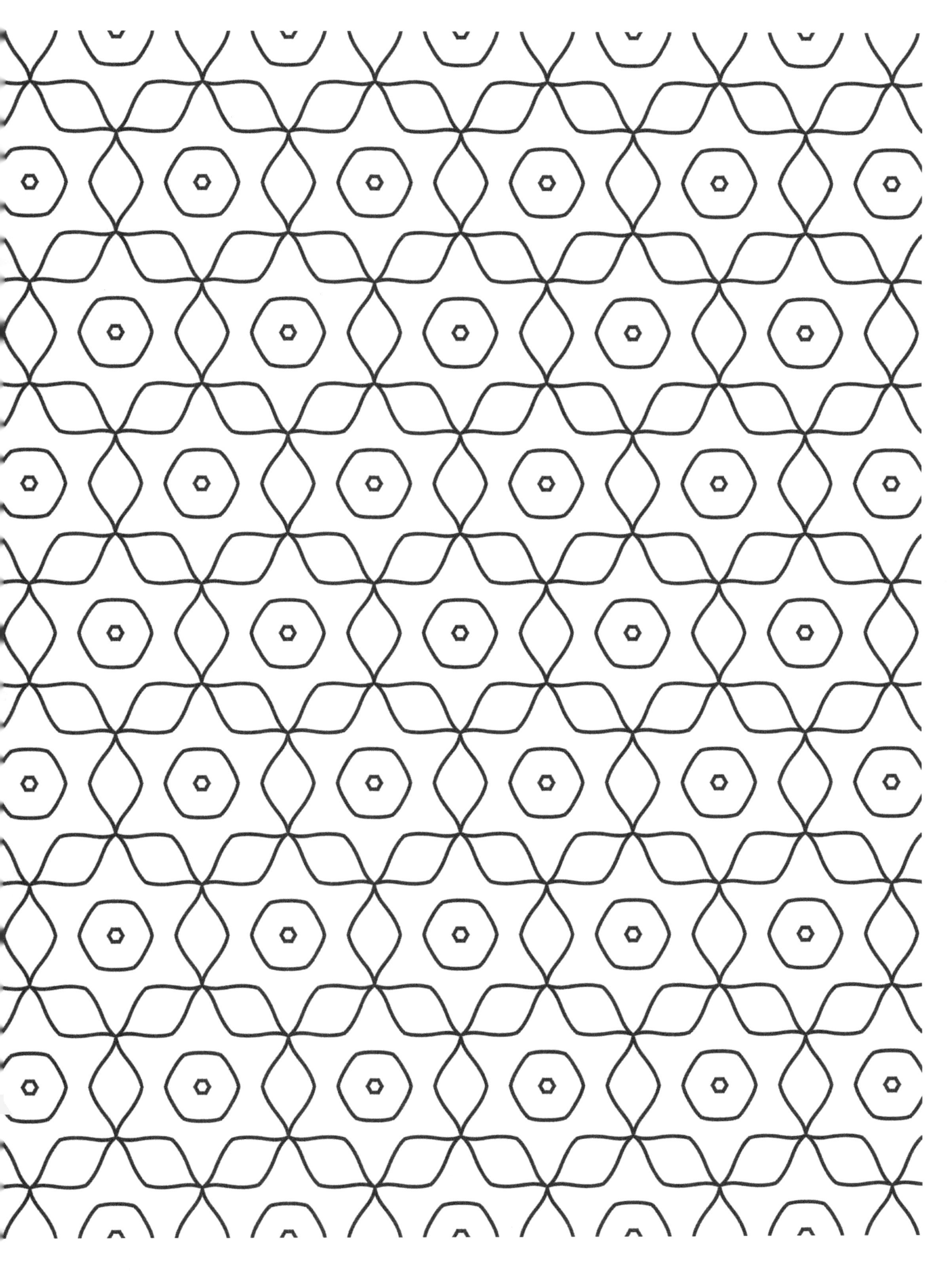

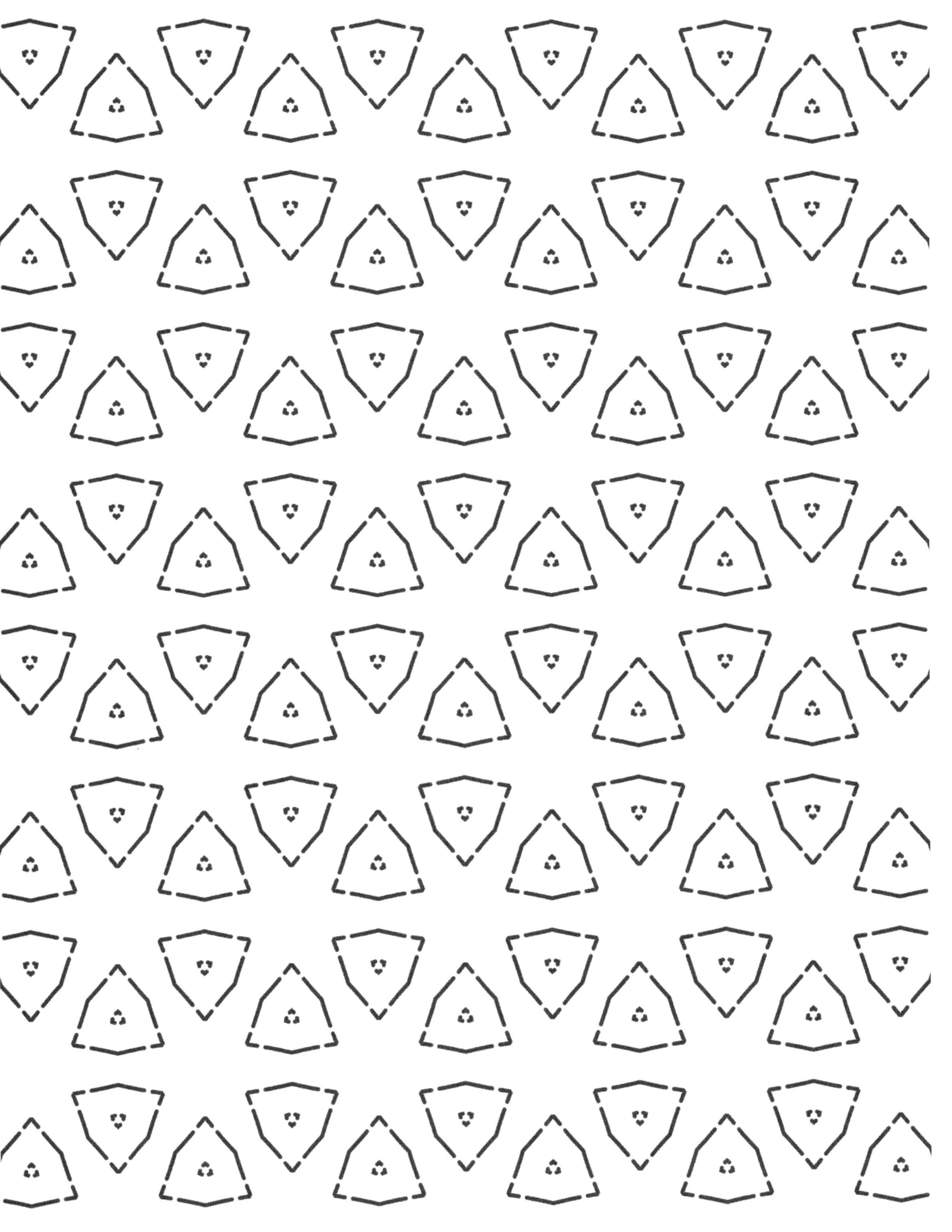

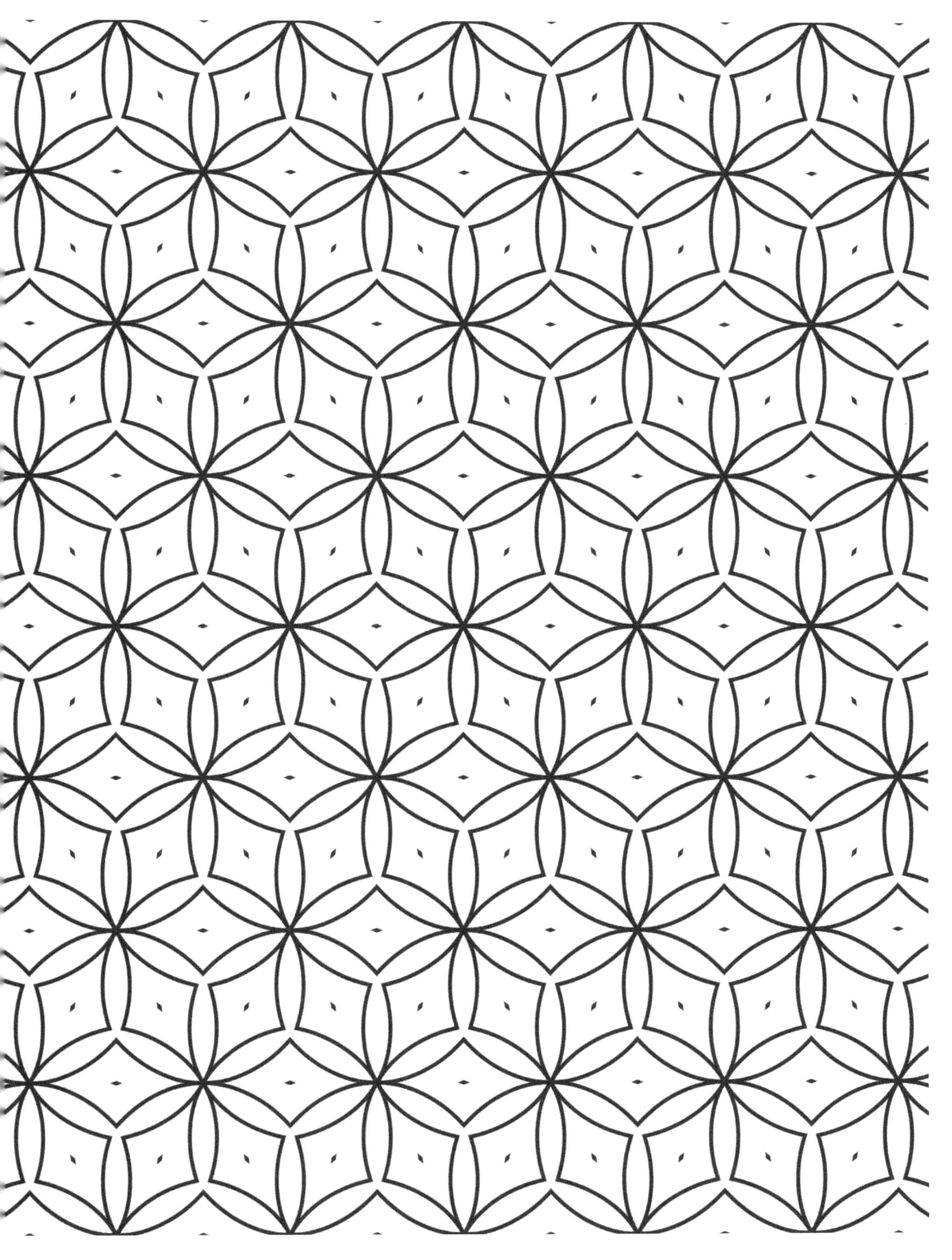

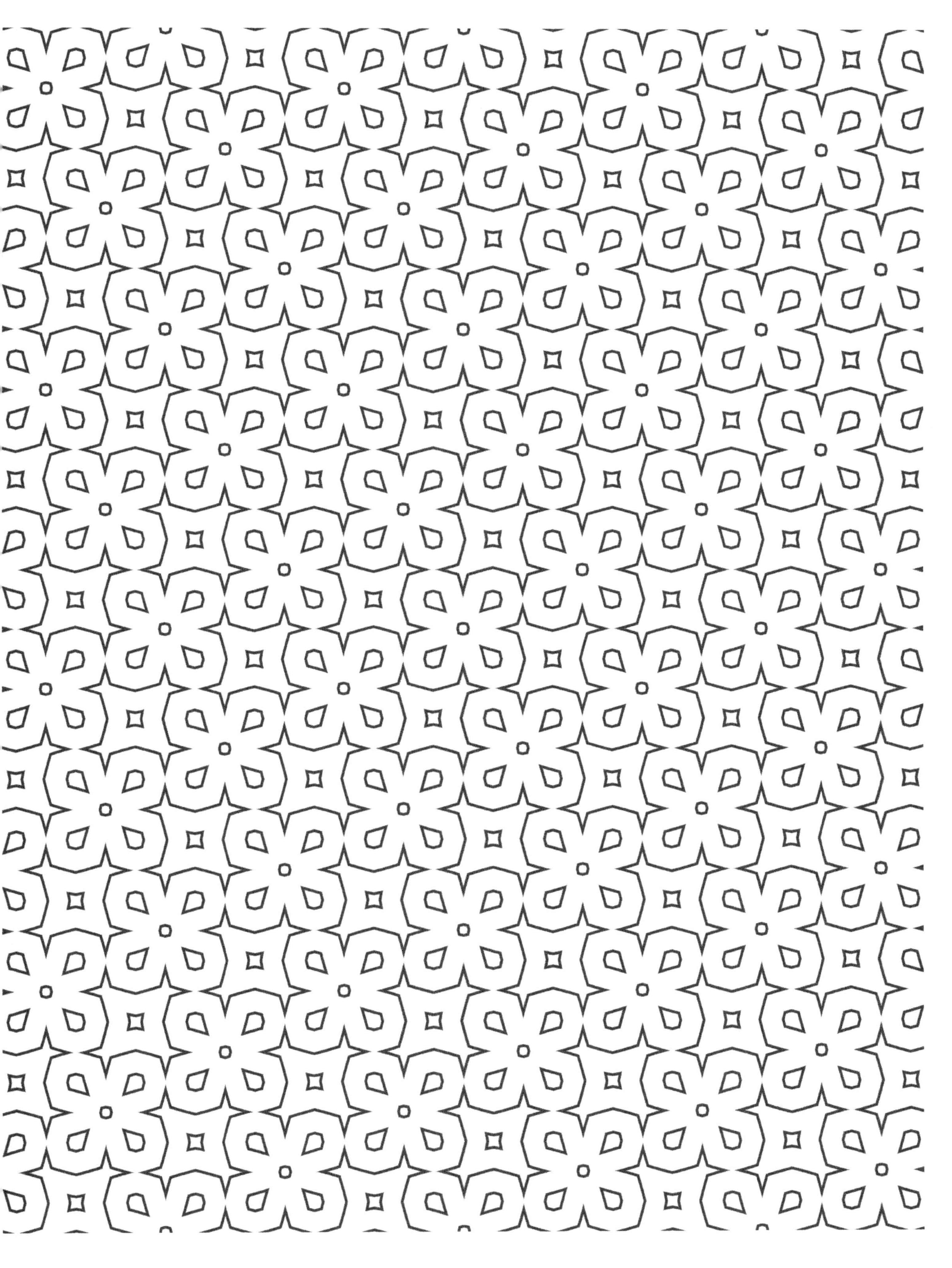

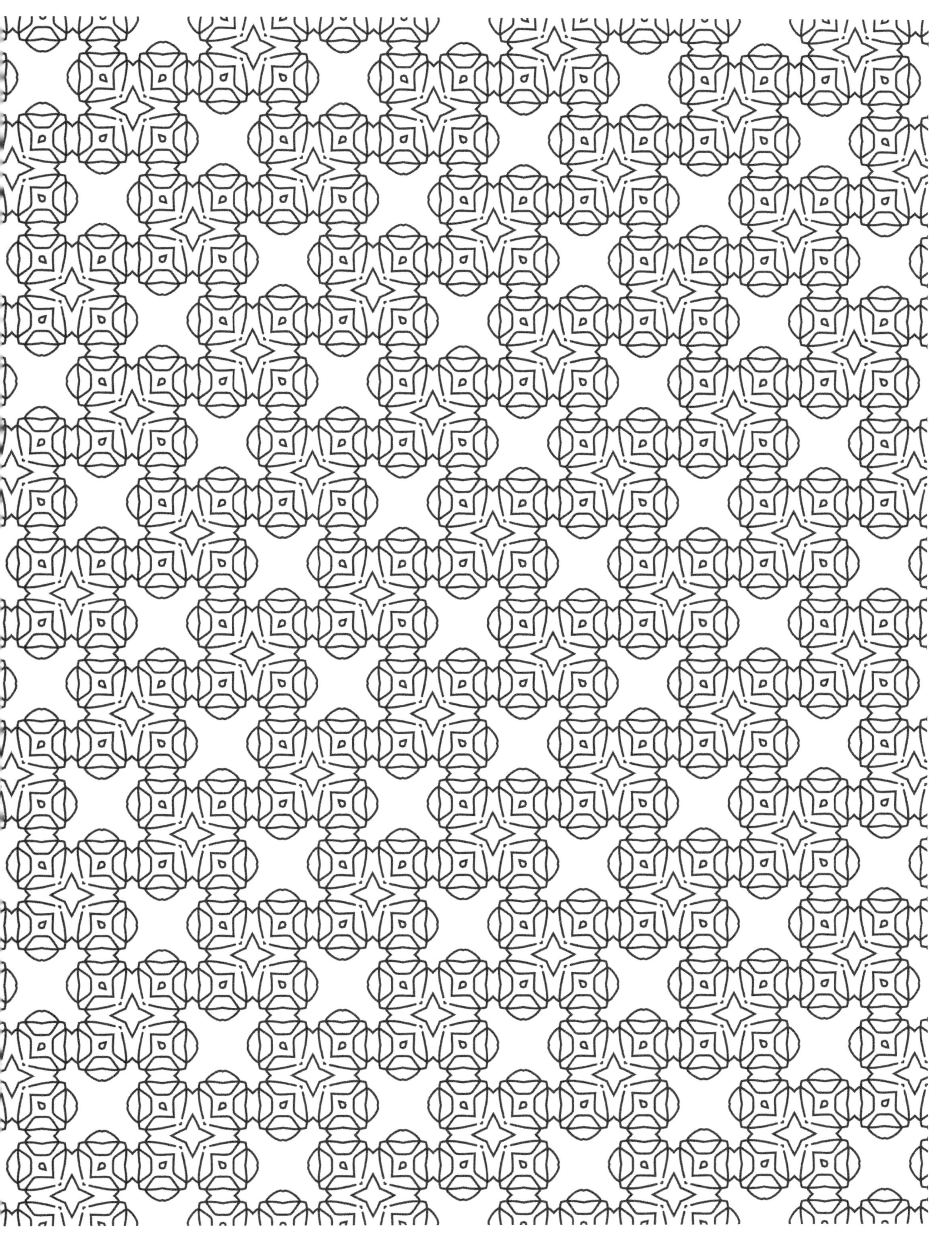

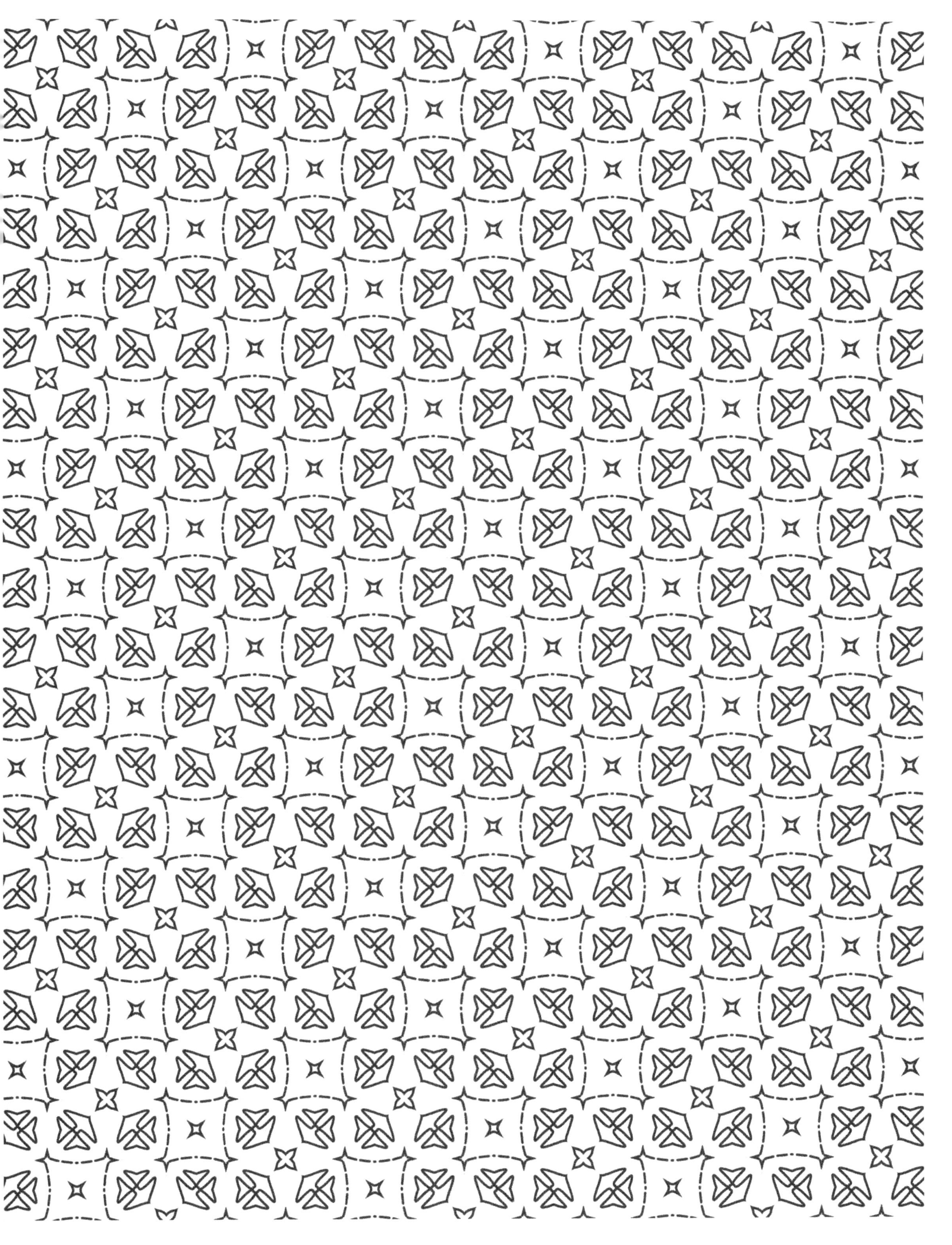

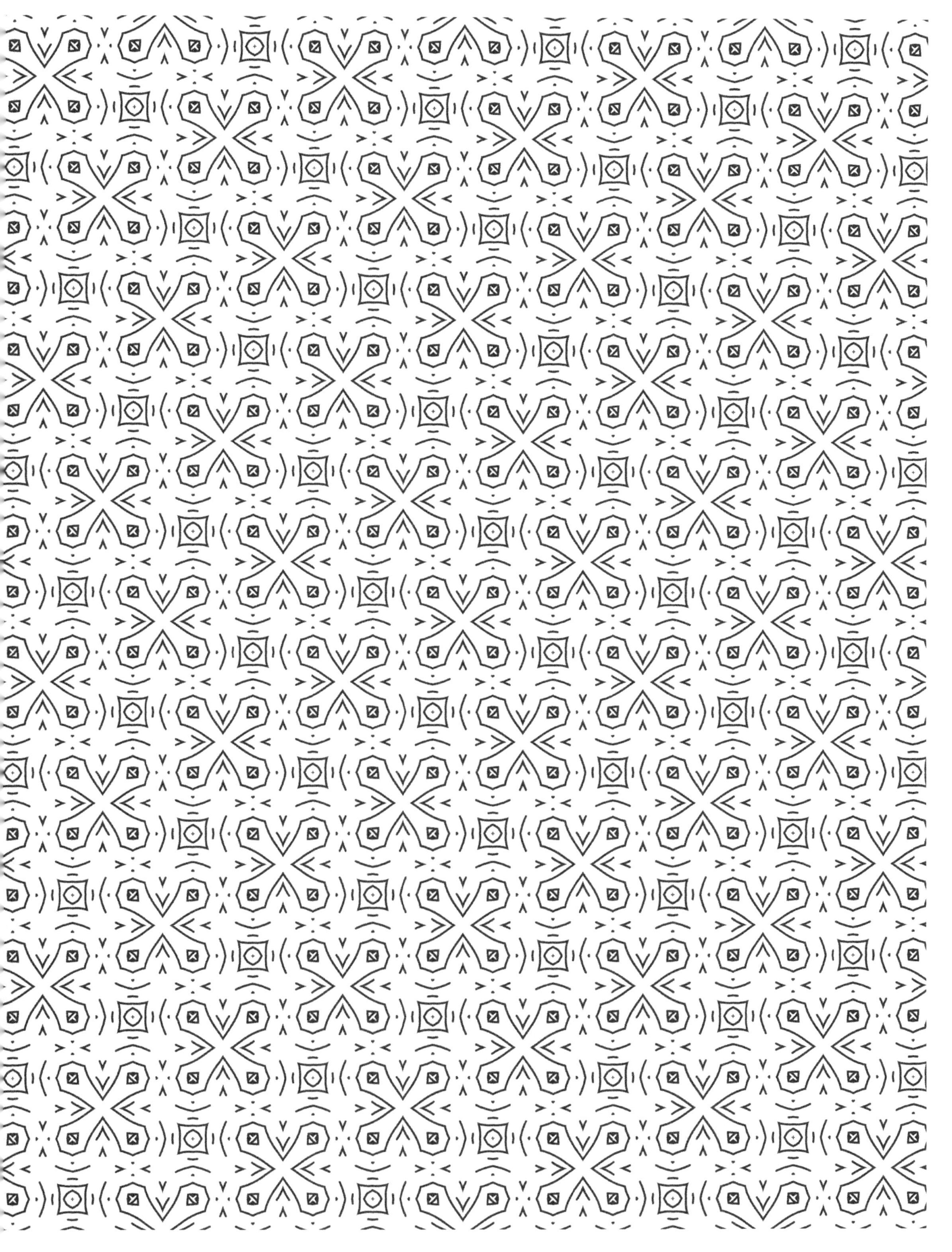

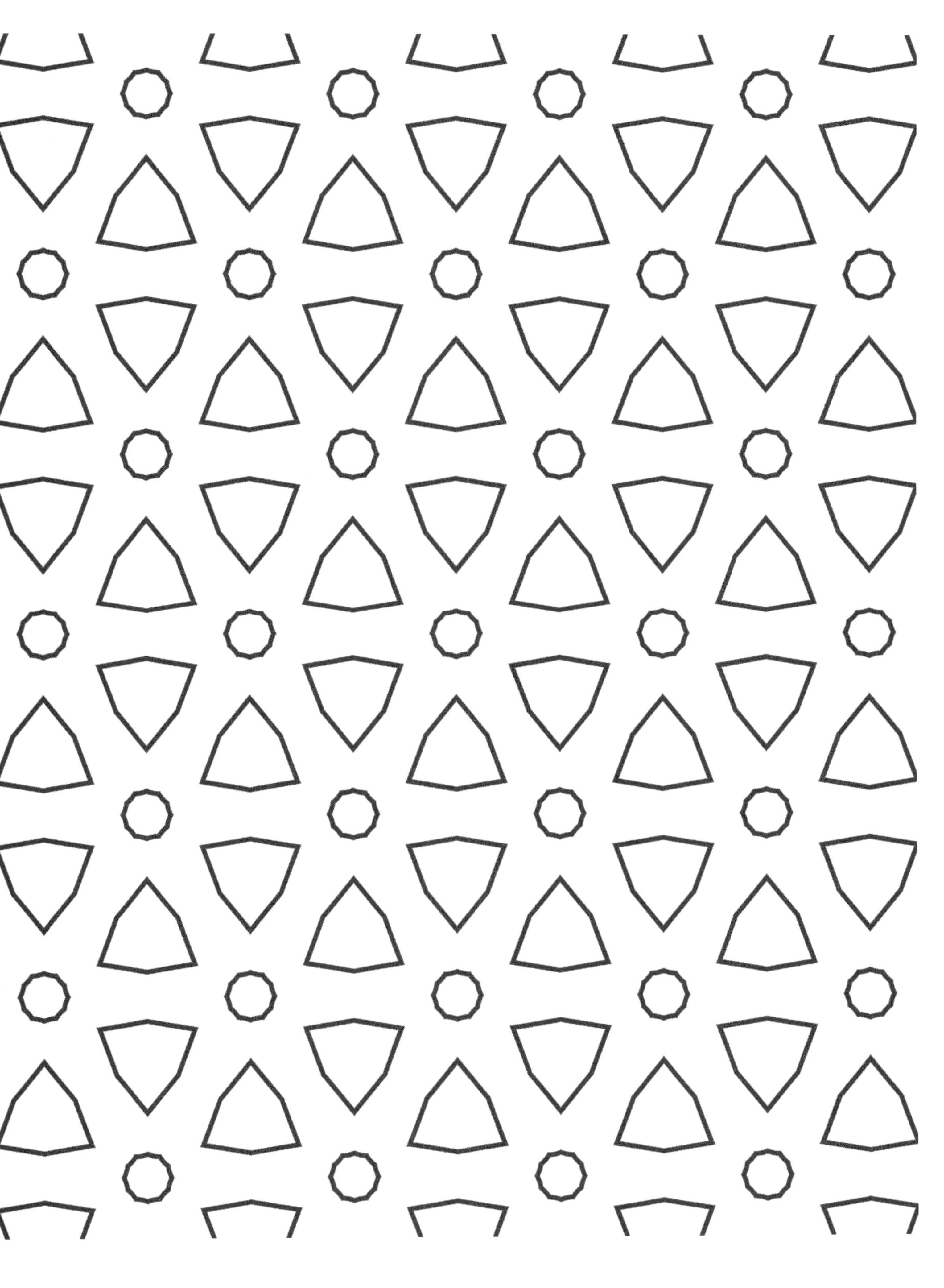

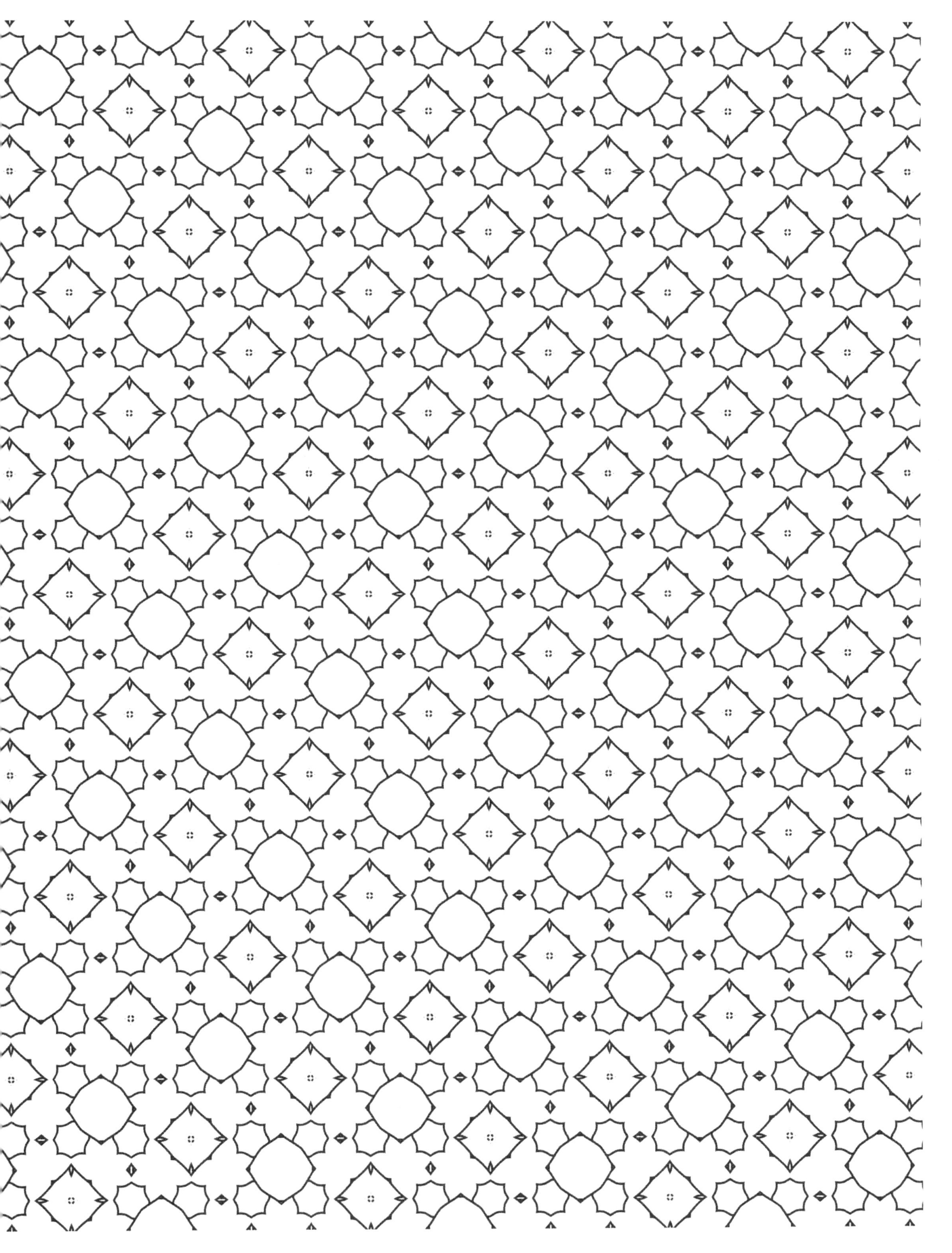

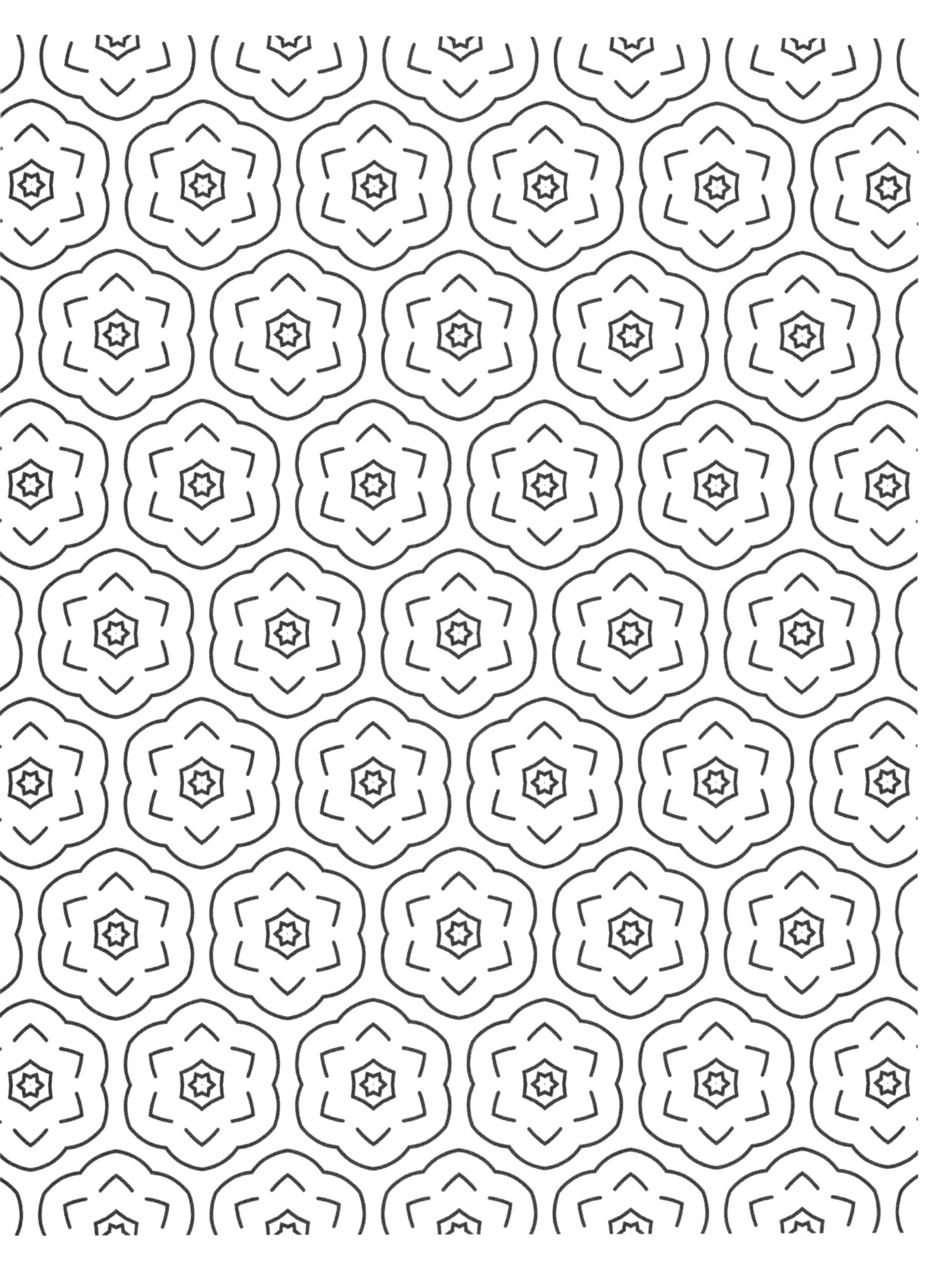

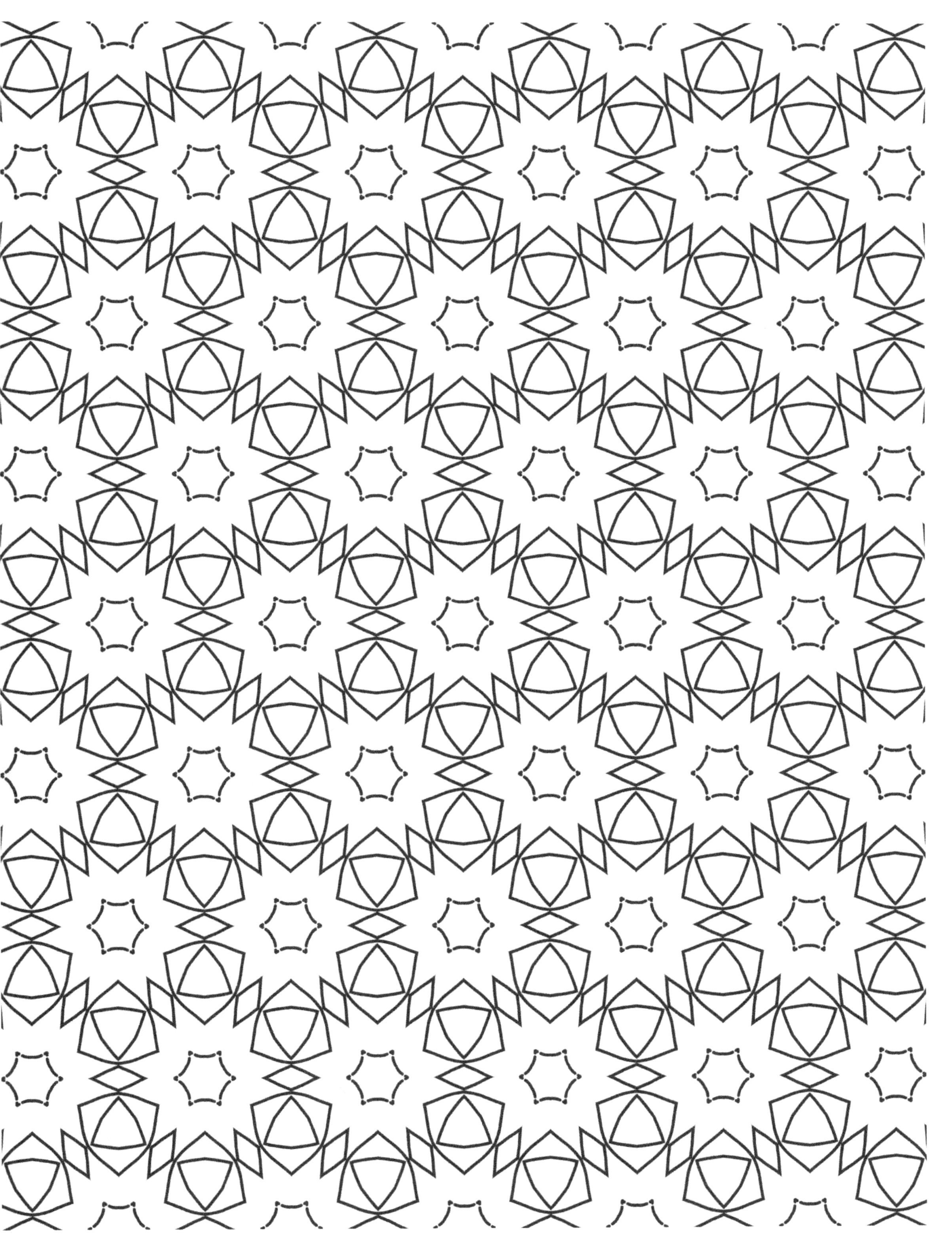

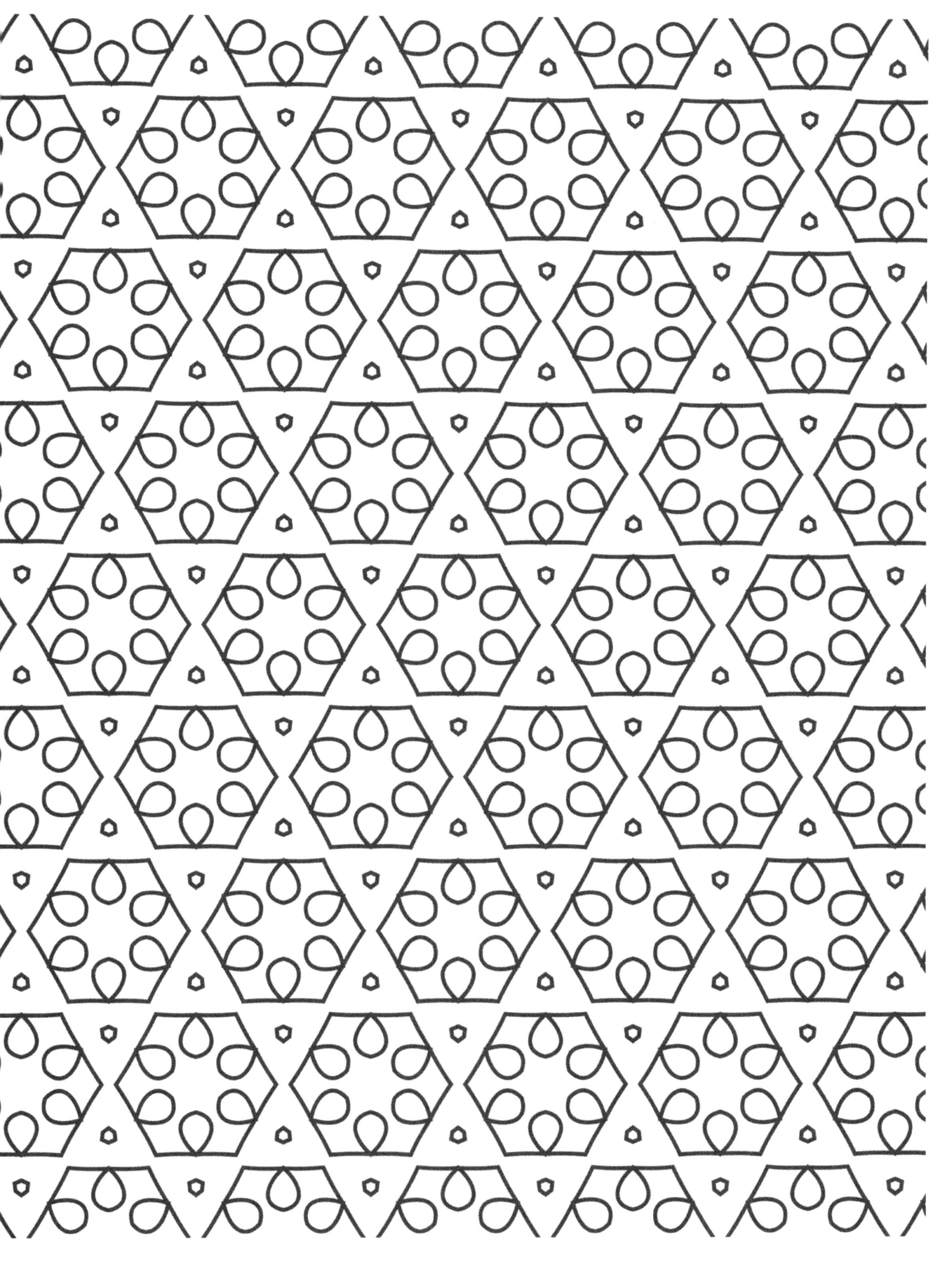

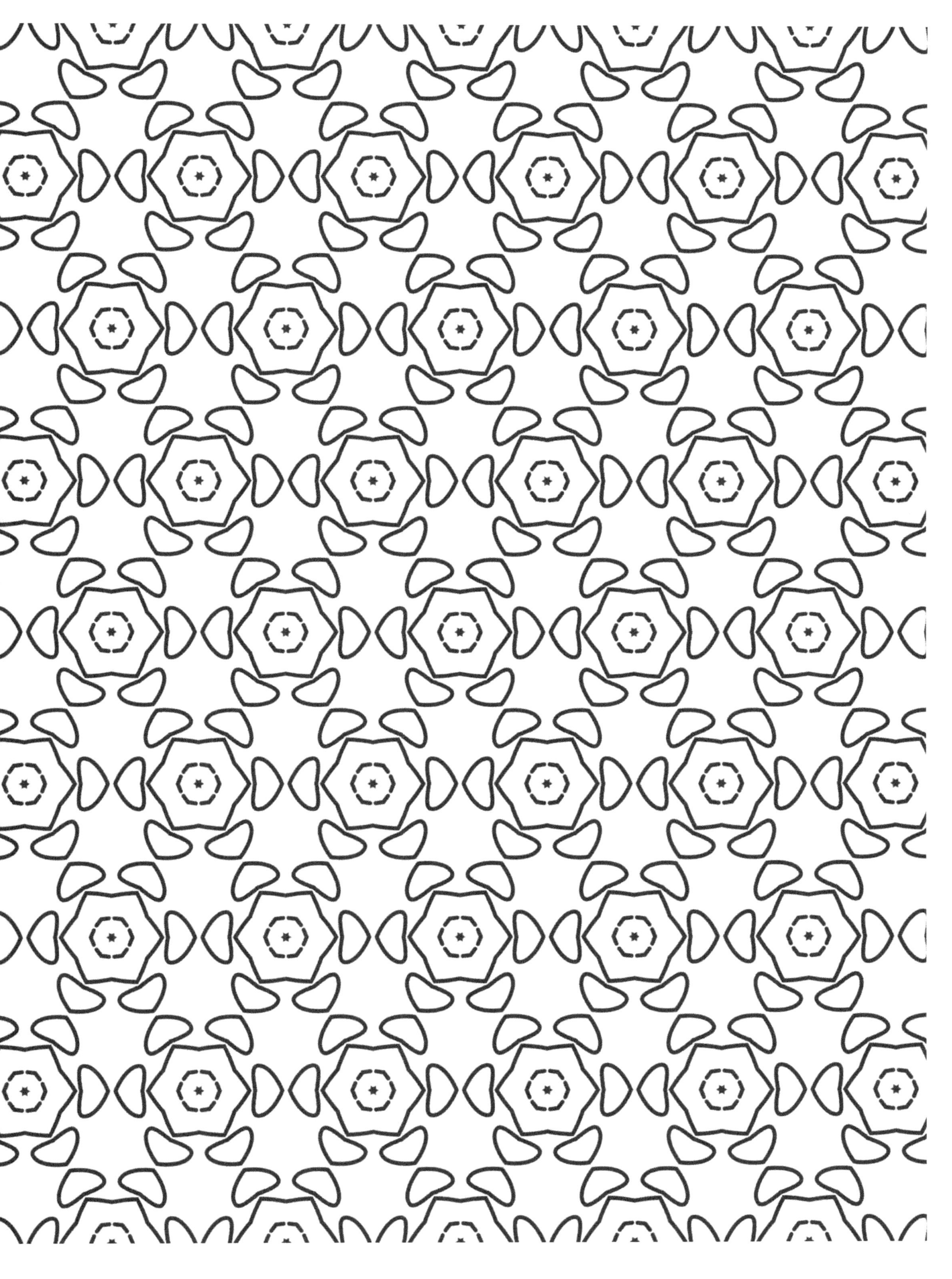

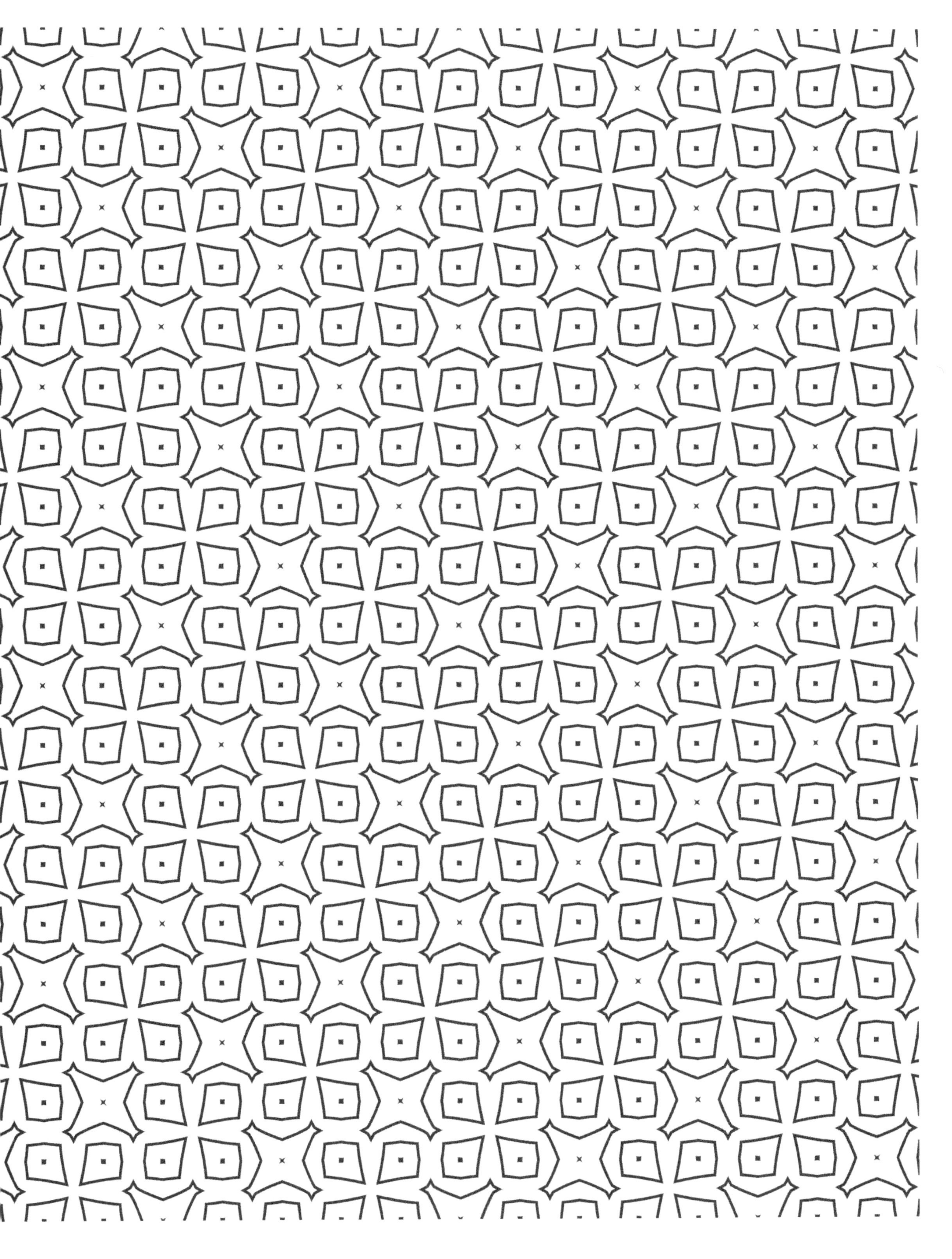

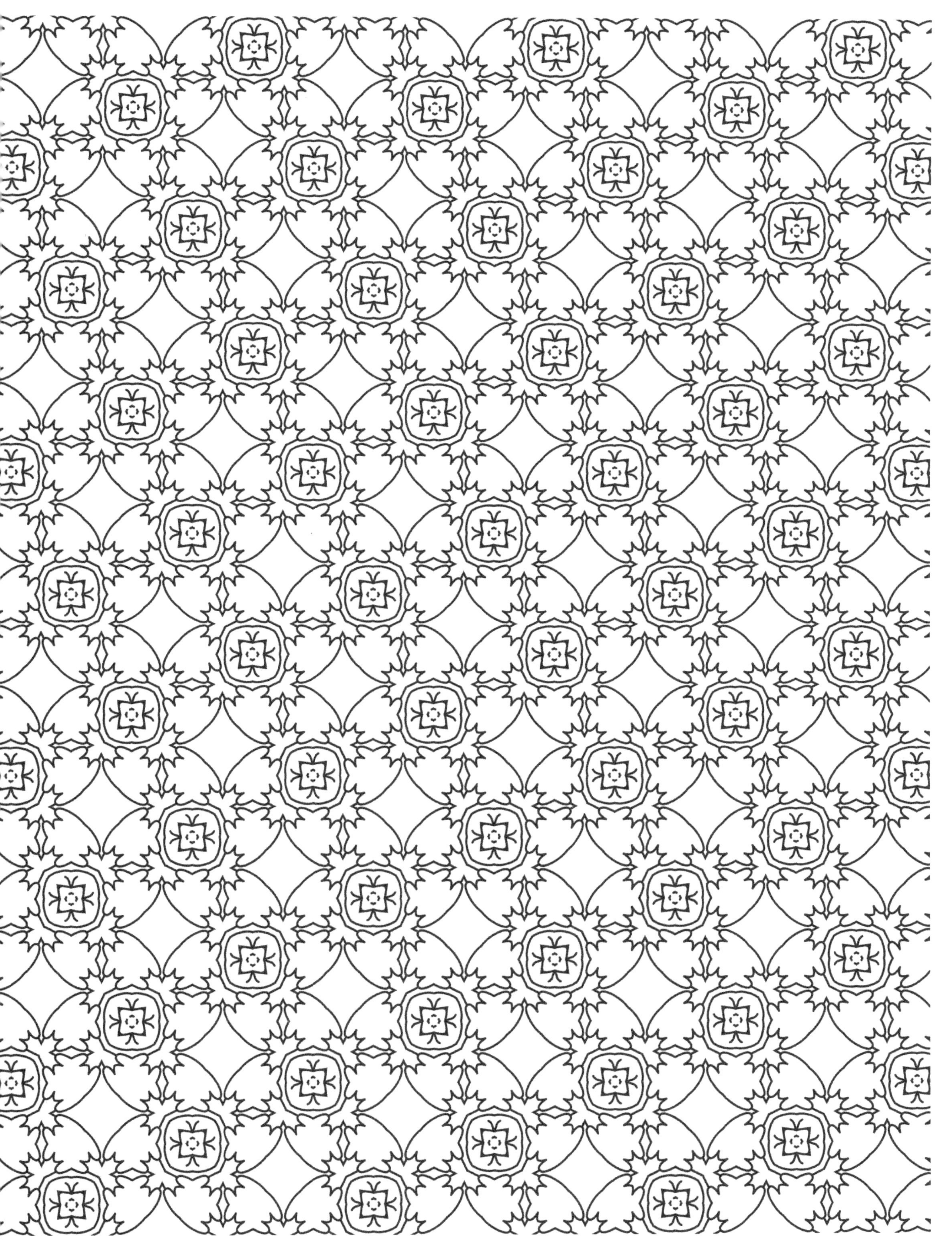

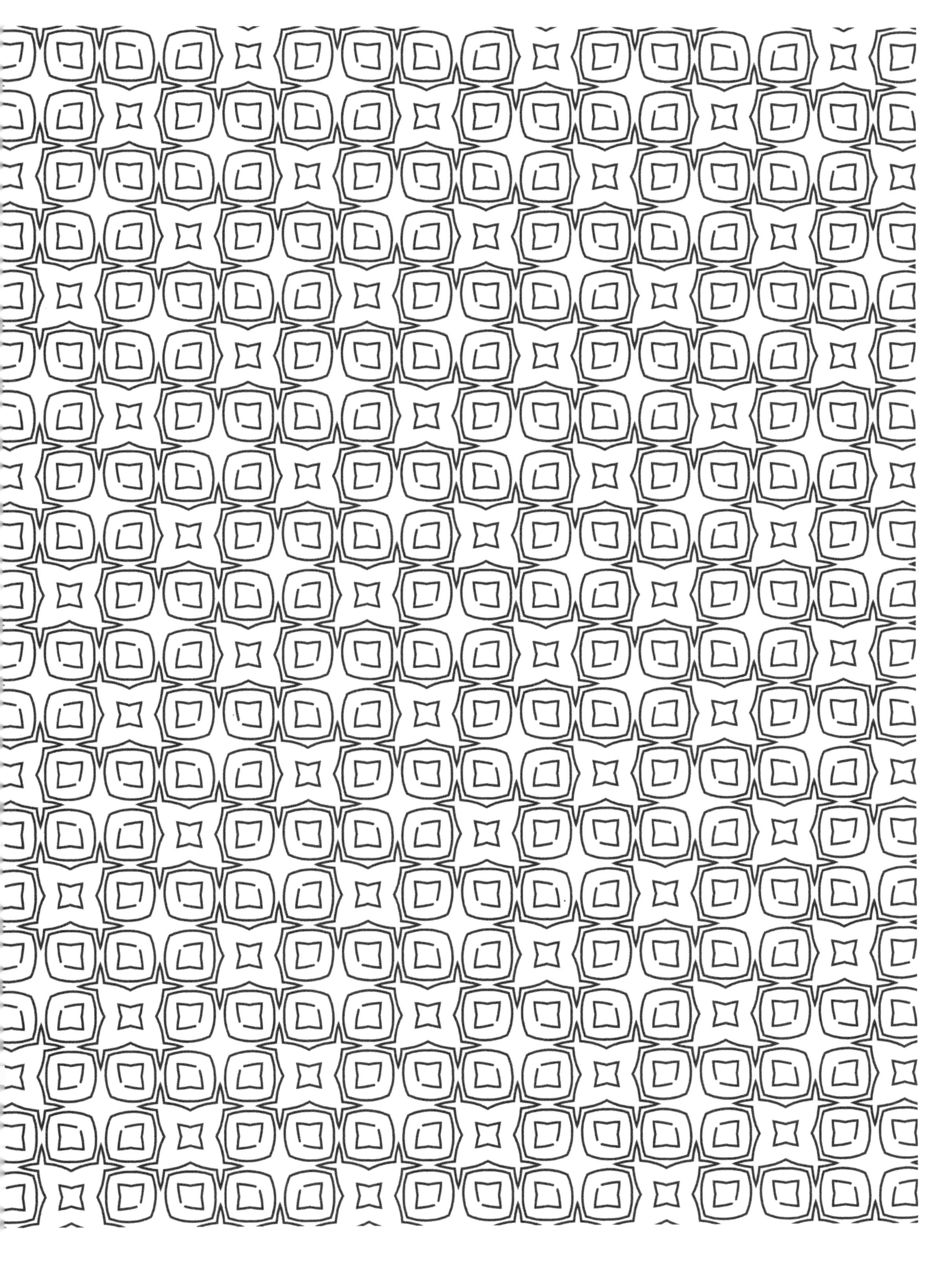

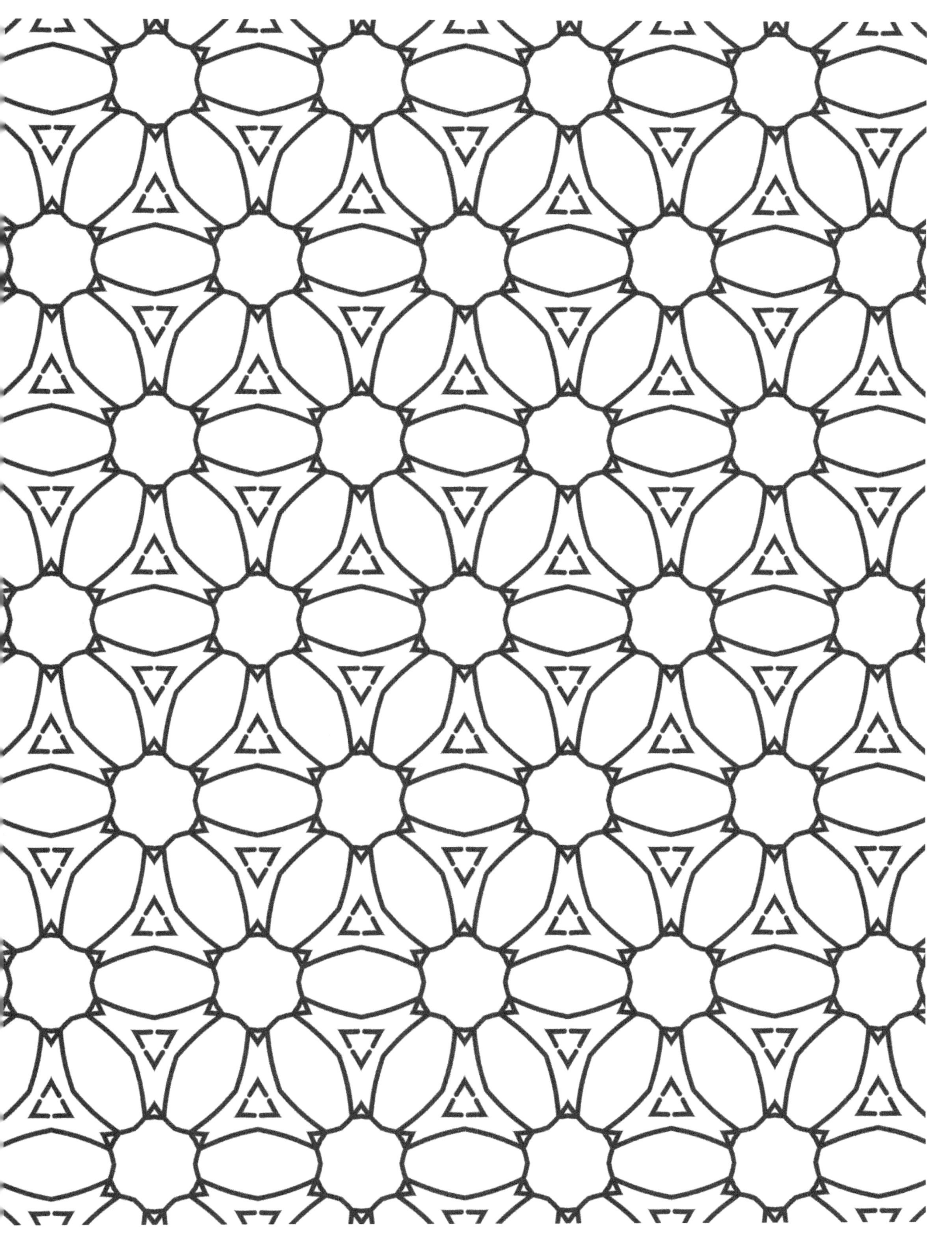

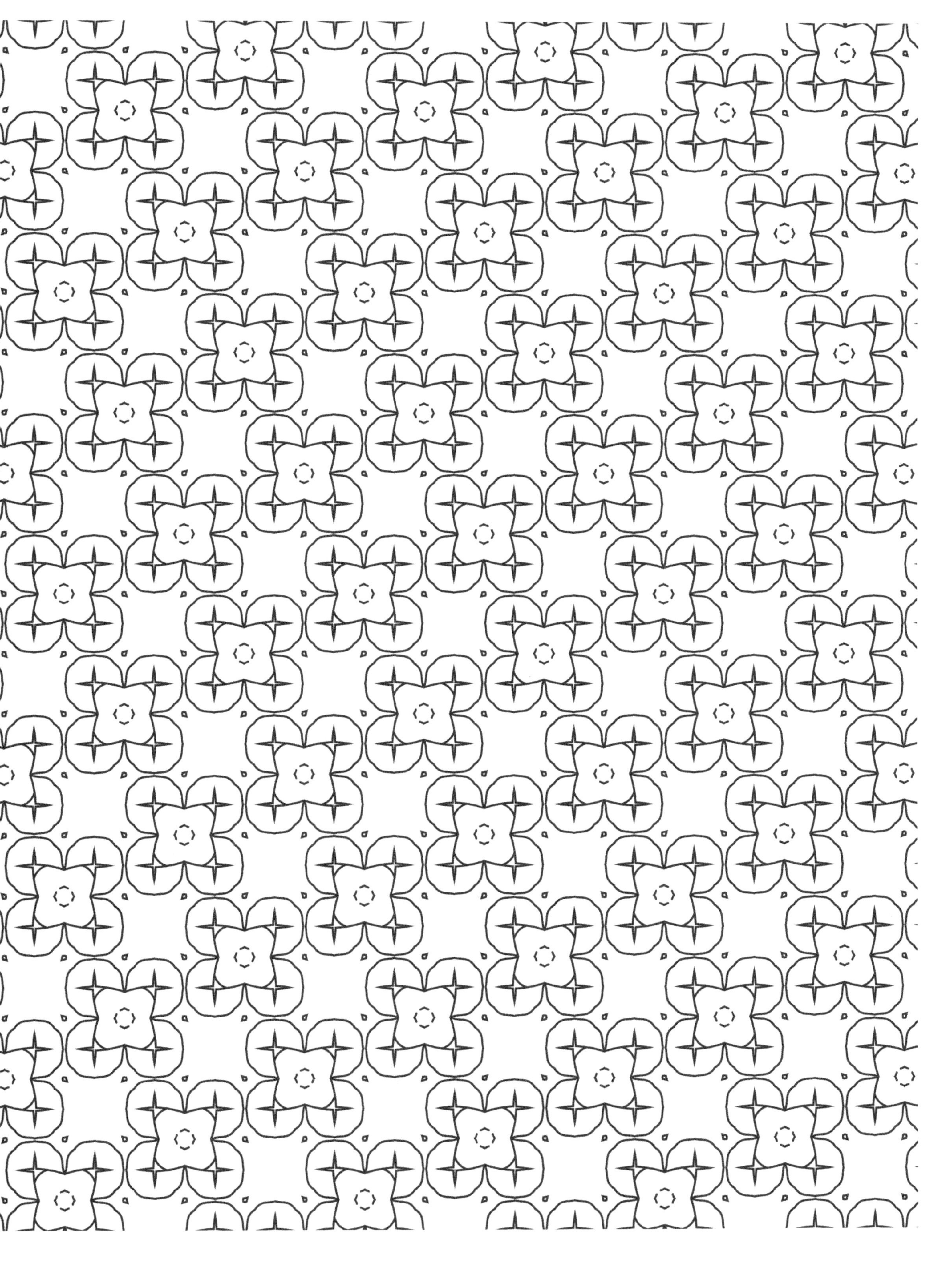

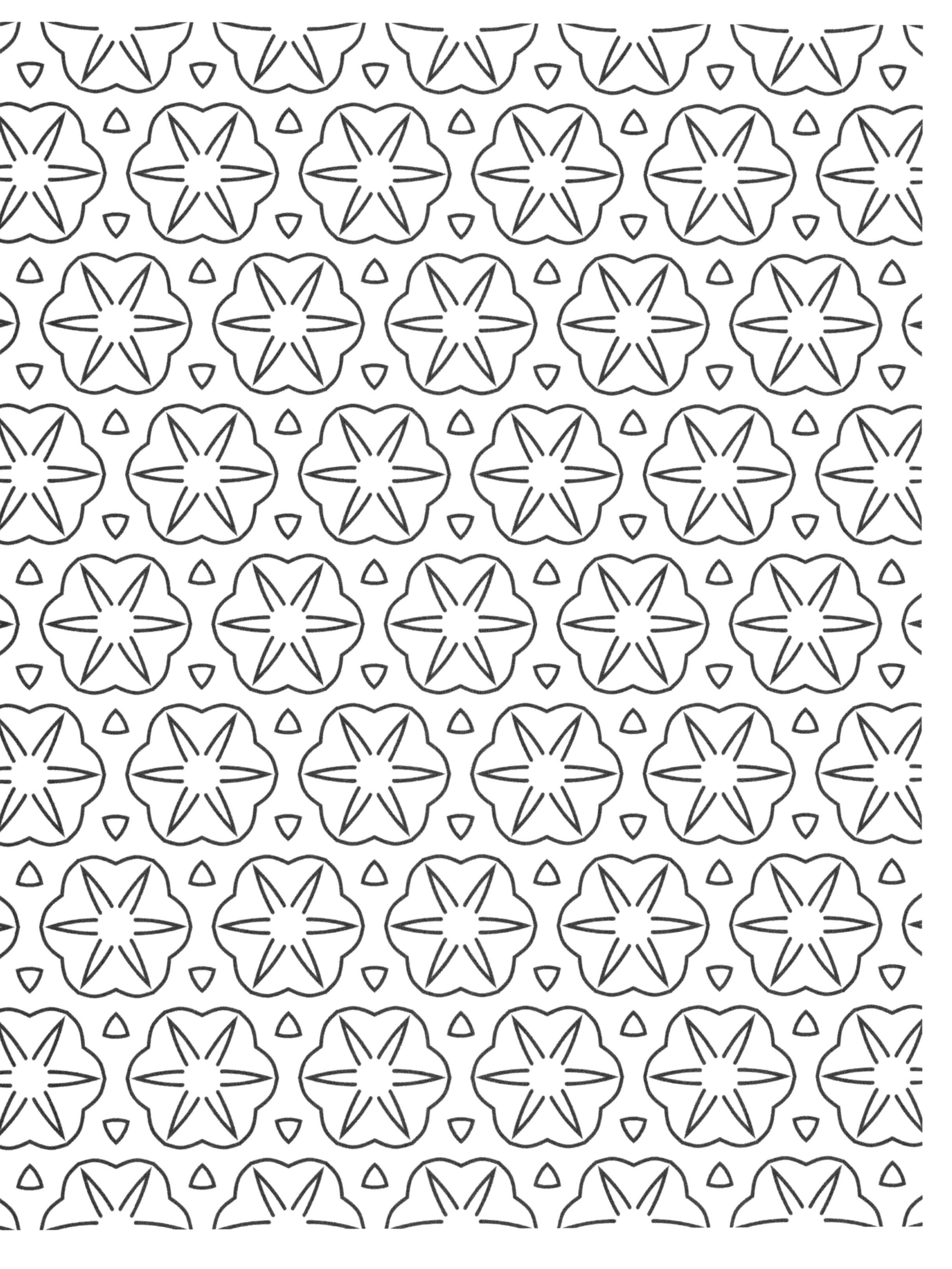

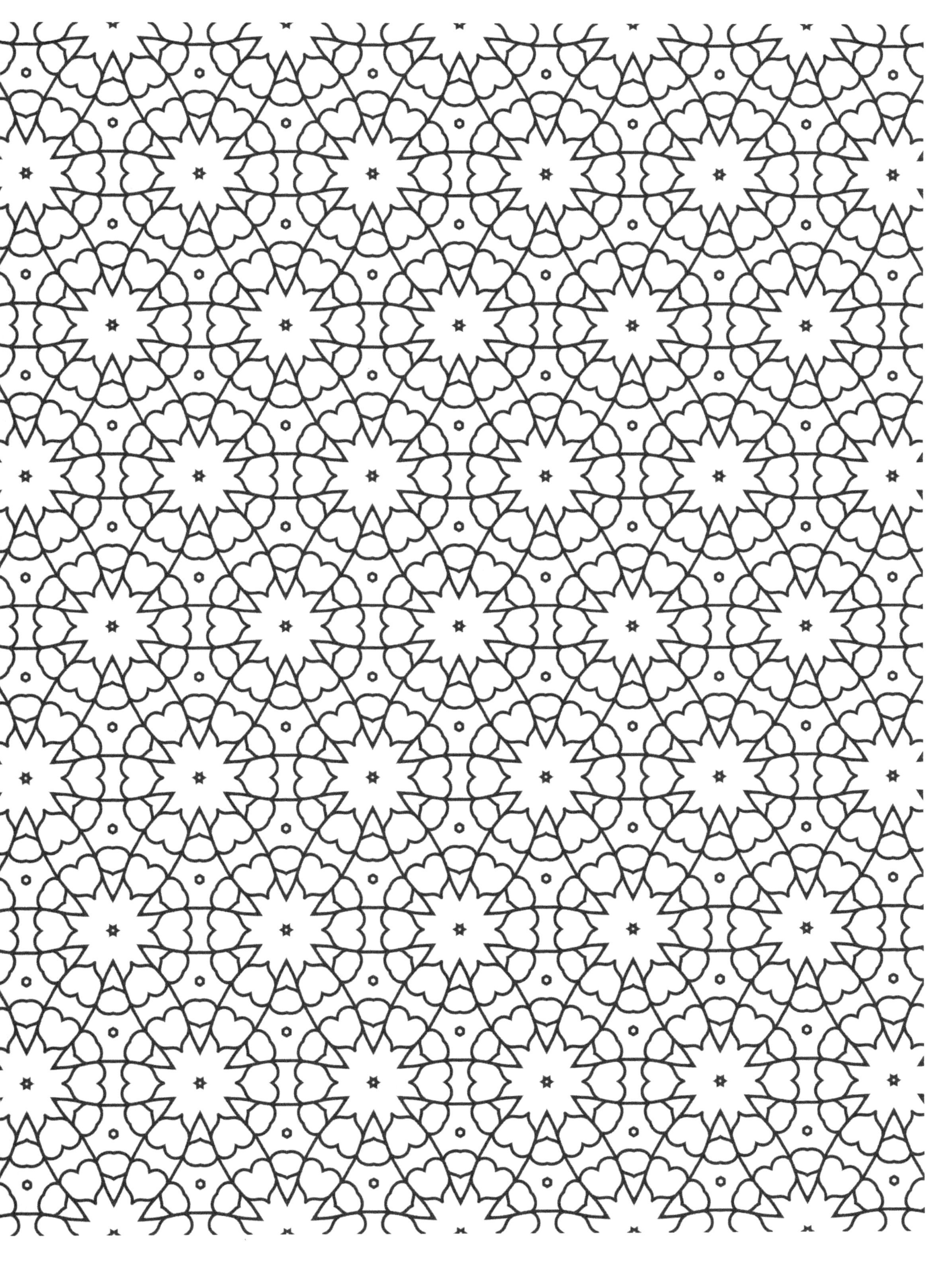

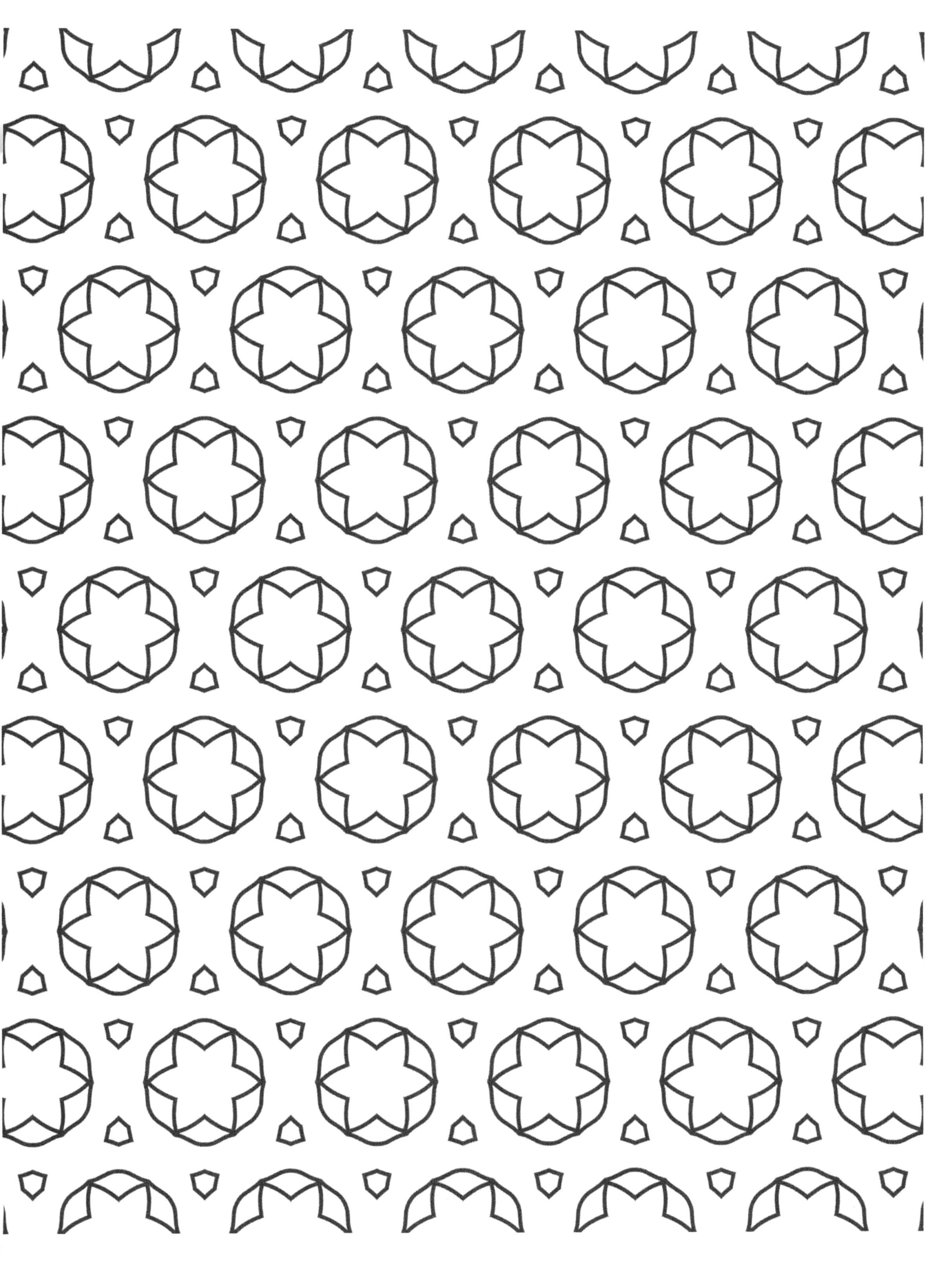